# Mary Cassatt

By Iain Zaczek

Gareth Stevens
PUBLISHING

Please visit our website, www.garethstevens.com. For a free color catalog of all our high-quality books, call toll-free 1-800-542-2595 or fax 1-877-542-2596.

**Library of Congress Cataloging-in-Publication Data**

Zaczek, Iain.
Mary Cassatt / by Iain Zaczek.
p. cm. — (Great artists)
Includes index.
ISBN 978-1-4824-1219-2 (pbk.)
ISBN 978-1-4824-1247-5 (6-pack)
ISBN 978-1-4824-1504-9 (library binding)
1. Cassatt, Mary, — 1844-1926 — Juvenile literature. 2. Artists — United States — Biography — Juvenile literature. I. Zaczek, Iain. II. Title.
N6537.C35 Z33 2015
759.13—d23                                          2012024372

**Published in 2015 by**
Gareth Stevens Publishing
111 East 14th Street, Suite 349
New York, NY 10003

For Brown Bear Books Ltd:
Editorial Director: Lindsey Lowe
Managing Editor: Tim Cooke
Children's Publisher: Anne O'Daly
Design Manager: Keith Davis
Designer: Supriya Sahai
Picture Manager: Sophie Mortimer

**Picture Credits**
Special thanks to The Art Archive
T=Top, C=Center, B=Bottom, L=Left, R=Right
Cover, ©The Art Archive/National Gallery of Art Washington/Superstock; FC t©Public Domain/Foundation of American Art: 4, ©Public Domain/National Portrait Gallery Washington; 5tr, ©Library of Congress; 6cl, ©Public Domain/Walters Art Museum; 6br, ©The Art Archive/National Gallery; 7, ©Public Domain/Deutsches Historischs Museum: 8, ©Public Domain/Metropolitan Museum of Art/Edouard Baldus; 9t, ©Public Domain/Laird & Lee Chicago; 10-11, ©The Art Archive/Ashmolean Museum; 11, ©The Art Archive/DeA Picture Library/G. Nimatallah; 12-13, ©The Art Archive/Musee d'Orsay/Superstock; 15, ©The Art Archive/DeA Picture Library; 17, ©The Art Archive/DeA Picture Library; 19, ©The Art Archive/Superstock; 21, ©The Art Archive/Superstock; 22-23, ©The Art Archive/National Gallery of Art Washington/Superstock; 24-25, ©The Art Archive/Philadelphia Museum of Art/Superstock; 26-27, ©Public Domain/Metropolitan Museum of Art; 27, ©The Tate Gallery.

Brown Bear Books has made every attempt to contact the copyright holder. If anyone has any information please contact licensing@brownbearbooks.co.uk

All artwork: © Brown Bear Books/Supriya Sahai

Manufactured in the United States of America

CPSIA compliance information: Batch #CS15GS. For further information contact Gareth Stevens, New York, New York at 1-800-542-2595.

# Contents

# Life Story

Mary Cassatt was an important artist. She was a woman painter at a time when most painters were men. And she was an American who lived and worked in France.

Mary Stevenson Cassatt was born on May 22, 1844, in Allegheny City, Pennsylvania. Her parents were wealthy. Her father, Robert Cassatt, was a banker. He also became mayor of Allegheny City. His family had originally come from France to America in the 17th century. Mary's mother, Katherine, loved the arts and reading books.

Birth name: **Mary Stevenson Cassatt**

Born: **May 22, 1844, Allegheny City, Pittsburgh, Pennsylvania, United States**

Died: **June 14, 1926, near Paris, France**

Nationality: **American**

Field: **Painting, printmaking**

Movement: **Impressionism**

Influenced by: **Impressionism, Edgar Degas, Édouard Manet, Gustave Courbet, Japanese printmaking**

***Mary Cassatt***
Edgar Degas (c.1880)

4

## Move to Europe

In 1851, the Cassatt family moved to Europe. They lived in France and then in Germany. Mary learned to speak French and German. She enjoyed the European lifestyle. In 1855, the Cassatts returned to the United States. On the way back, they stopped in Paris. They saw an exhibition of paintings by French artists such as Ingres, Delacroix, Degas, and Pissarro.

## Art Classes

In 1861, Mary joined an art class at the Pennsylvania Academy of Fine Arts in Philadelphia. It was not unusual for a woman to be interested in art. But in 1865, Mary made a decision that was very unusual. She decided to study art in Europe. Her family tried to stop her, but Mary was determined to go. In 1866, Mary and her mother returned to Paris.

### Famous Paintings:
- *Young Woman Sewing in a Garden* 1880–1882
- *At the Opéra* 1879
- *The Child's Bath* 1893
- *The Boating Party* 1893–1894
- *"Set of Ten" Prints* 1890–1891

If painting is no longer needed, it seems a pity that some of us are born into the world with such a passion for line and color.

## WOMEN AT WORK

Before Mary, two other American women had moved to Europe to become artists. In 1853, Harriet Hosmer went to Rome, Italy. She became a sculptor. Edmonia Lewis also studied sculpture in Rome. In 1868, US President Ulysses S. Grant asked her to make a stone portrait of his head.

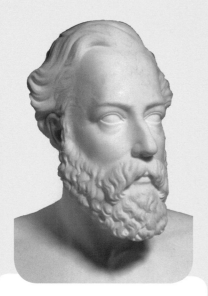

**Edmonia Lewis** made this bust of Dio Lewis, a famous American doctor, in 1868.

## Exciting City

Paris was an exciting city. It attracted many artists. Most painted traditional subjects. But there were also many who were trying new ideas. An artist named Édouard Manet was painting scenes of everyday life. Other artists were also trying new ways of painting.

Mary had lessons in art. At first she copied old pictures in galleries and museums. This was how many artists learned to paint. But she also picked up some new ideas. In 1868, she had a painting accepted by the Paris Salon. This was an exhibition of the best paintings in France. But in 1870, France went to war with its neighbor, Prussia (now part of Germany). Mary moved back to Philadelphia until the war was over.

## A New Home

In 1874, after traveling and painting in Italy and Spain, Mary decided to settle in Paris. The decision changed her life. The same year a group of young artists staged their own exhibition there. These artists were named the "Impressionists." They wanted to paint things as they really looked.

## OLD MASTERS

In Italy and Spain, Mary studied the works of great painters, such as the Spanish artist Goya. Goya painted Doña Isabel de Porcel in 1805.

**FRANCE AT WAR**
The Franco–Prussian War interrupted Mary's studies in Paris. She returned to the United States until it was over.

Mary was excited by their methods. She began using paler colors and painting outdoors, which was unusual. She made important new friends. One was an American art collector named Louisine Waldron Elder (later Havemeyer). Mary persuaded her to buy pictures painted by the Impressionists.

Mary's own paintings were beginning to attract attention from the Impressionists. When Degas saw one of her paintings he said, "There is someone who feels as I do." Mary met Degas in 1877. They became friends. Degas asked Mary to exhibit her paintings with the Impressionists. For the first time, Mary felt she could paint what she liked. She did not have to worry about the judges at the Paris Salon.

**Important people**

**Edgar Degas** – friend, artist

**Katherine Kelso Cassatt** – mother

**Édouard Manet** – friend, artist

**Louisine Havemeyer** – friend, art collector

"I hated conventional art. I began to live."

Mary's paintings were included in four Impressionist exhibitions. She was becoming famous. Her pictures were often paintings of people. She painted members of her own family when they visited Paris.

## Growing Fame

In the 1890s, Mary worked hard. She began to make prints as well as paintings. She created designs that could be copied many times. Now, she became famous in the United States. In 1892, she was asked to paint a mural for the "Women's Building" at the 1893 World's Columbian Exposition in Chicago. Mary painted *Modern Woman*, a huge work that was 50 feet (15 m) long.

Mary was now wealthy enough to buy the 17th-century Château de Beaufresne outside Paris. It became her summer home.

### The Impressionists

**The Impressionists held their first exhibition in Paris in 1874. They were a group of young artists who wanted to paint in a new way. The Impressionists often painted outside. They tried to paint things as they really looked.**

**Mary lived in Paris for nearly 50 years. The city was famous for its artists. Many of the world's best painters lived there.**

**The Women's Building** at the World's Columbian Exposition in Chicago where Mary painted her huge mural *Modern Woman.*

In 1895, Mary's mother died. Mary went back to visit her family in the United States for the first time in 25 years. But Mary soon returned to France.

## Mothers and Babies

In the 1900s, Mary spent a lot of time with Louisine. Mary advised Louisine and her husband on what paintings to buy for their art collection. Mary was also asked to paint portraits of mothers and their children. This subject had become her specialty. In 1904, the French government awarded her the Légion d'Honneur medal for services to art.

By 1910, Mary was becoming sick. She could not paint much any more. Her eyesight was failing. Mary died at the Château de Beaufresne in June 1926.

## Important places

**Allegheny City – Pennsylvania**

**Pittsburgh – Pennsylvania**

**Parma – Italy**

**Seville – Spain**

**Paris – France**

**Chicago –Illinois**

Cézanne doesn't believe that everyone should see alike.

# How Cassatt Painted

Mary began painting in a traditional way. Later, she was influenced by the Impressionists and by Japanese printmakers.

At the start of her career, Mary traveled widely and studied the work of painters from the past. She particularly liked the work of the Spaniard Diego Velázquez (1599–1660) and the Flemish artist Peter Paul Rubens (1577–1640).

In 1877, Mary met the Impressionist Edgar Degas. Mary began to paint scenes from modern, everyday life. She often painted outdoors.

### Japanese prints

Mary liked the style of Japanese artists. They made prints that could be copied on a printing press. The shapes seem simple, but the sizes of things in this landscape by the artist Hiroshige do not seem lifelike. This boat looks big compared to the shore.

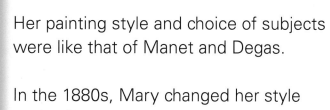

Her painting style and choice of subjects were like that of Manet and Degas.

In the 1880s, Mary changed her style again. She became known for her portraits of women and children. In the 1890s, she began to make prints. She had been inspired by Japanese woodblock prints and drypoint engraving. Mary's paintings changed, too. Her figures appear more solid and have clear outlines. She also began to use bold colors.

## Important French Painters

**Paul Cézanne**

**Gustave Courbet**

**Edgar Degas**

**Édouard Manet**

**Jean-François Millet**

**Claude Monet**

**Camille Pissarro**

**Pierre-Auguste Renoir**

# Young Woman Sewing in a Garden

Mary painted this picture between 1880 and 1882. It is in the style of the Impressionists. The painting was shown in the last exhibition by the Impressionists in 1886.

**The girl** looks serious. Her face is drawn in detail. The plants behind her are more like impressions of flowers and trees.

Mary's painting was unusual. The girl is at the front of the picture, so she looks big. There isn't room to fit her whole dress into the painting. Her position is straight and upright, like the tree behind her. This makes the girl stand out from the swirling background. The slanting path gives the picture a feeling of space or distance.

## In the Frame

🖌 The original painting of *Young Woman Sewing in a Garden* is 36 inches (92 cm) tall and 25.5 inches (65 cm) wide.

🖌 Cassatt often painted images of women and children in everyday settings.

🖌 The painting was done in oil on canvas.

## CASSATT'S
### Palette of the picture

**The edges** of the girl's skirt are blurred. This style of painting was popular with the Impressionists.

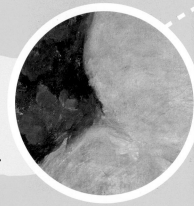

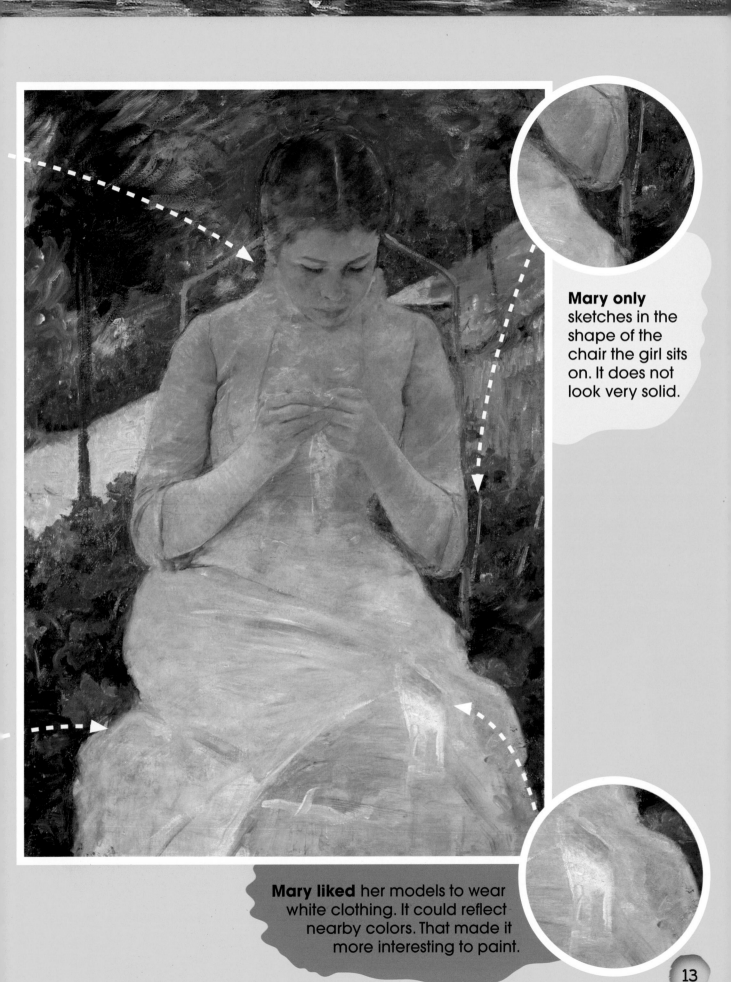

**Mary only** sketches in the shape of the chair the girl sits on. It does not look very solid.

**Mary liked** her models to wear white clothing. It could reflect nearby colors. That made it more interesting to paint.

# At the Opéra

Mary painted this picture of a woman at the theater in Paris in 1879. The theater was a popular subject for Impressionist artists. Degas and Renoir both painted scenes in theaters.

**The other** people at the theater are only shown as shapes. There is no detail in their faces.

The woman is attending a matinee, or afternoon performance. It is the interval, so the theater lights are on. The woman is not looking down at the stage. She is looking through her opera glasses (small binoculars) at other people in the audience. She does not know that a man in another box is looking at her. Matinees had been introduced in 1869. They were popular with women.

### In the Frame

🌷 The original painting of *At the Opéra* is 31.9 inches (81 cm) tall and 26 inches (66 cm) wide.

🌷 The model for the picture was Mary's sister, Lydia.

🌷 The original painting is in the Museum of Fine Arts, Boston, Massachusetts.

I am independent! I can live alone and I love to work.

**This man** leans over the balcony to stare at the woman through his opera glasses. Theaters were places where people liked to look at each other.

**The woman** is staring at someone outside the picture frame. Mary doesn't show us who it is.

**The woman** is dressed in daytime clothes. This shows that this is an afternoon matinee performance.

# The Child's Bath

Mary painted this picture in 1893. A few years earlier she had visited a major exhibition of Japanese prints in Paris. The prints gave her some ideas to use in her own paintings.

Mary's picture uses an unusual viewpoint, or angle. We are looking down on the woman and child. The figures have strong, clear shapes and outlines. The woman could be the mother of the little girl, but children in wealthy families were often bathed by a maid. However, by the 1880s, mothers began to spend more time with their children.

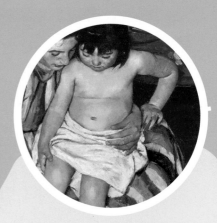

**Mary was** skilled at painting children in natural poses, or positions. The little girl supports herself on the woman's knee.

## CASSATT'S

**Palette of the picture**

## In the Frame

🖌 The original painting of *The Child's Bath* is 39.5 inches (100 cm) tall and 26 inches (66 cm) wide.

🖌 Mary often painted children and their parents or nursemaids.

🖌 The original painting is in the Art Institute of Chicago in Chicago, Illinois.

**The two** figures are looking down. That takes our eyes down to the main part of the picture.

**Mary liked** to paint her figures at the front of pictures. They often seem huge. This woman only just fits into the frame.

**Mary used** different angles in her pictures. The top of the jug is seen from slightly above, but the pattern is seen from the side.

17

# The Letter

**Mary's inspiration** for this picture is clear. This woman could easily be Japanese.

Mary's most unusual pictures were her prints. This print comes from a series of color prints known as the "Set of Ten." They are Mary's most famous prints. She exhibited them together in 1891.

Mary's prints were based on Japanese prints she had seen. She also used ideas from her friend Edgar Degas, who was also a good printmaker. To make a print, Mary scratched a picture on a plate of copper. She added ink to the surface. Then she pressed paper against the plate to make the print. Mary used a technique called aquatint to add color. She coated parts of the copper plate with colored powder as well as ink. It gave more variety to the print.

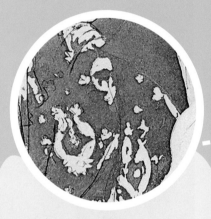

**Mary loved** the colors and decoration of Japanese prints. She spent a lot of time on the detail of the pattern on the woman's dress.

## CASSATT'S

### Palette of the picture

## In the Frame

🖌 The original print of *The Letter* is 13.5 inches (34.4 cm) tall and 8.3 inches (21.1 cm) wide.

🖌 The desk in the print belonged to the Cassatt family.

**This detail** would have seemed modern to Mary's audience. Envelopes sealed with sticky gum were quite new at the time.

**The edges** of the writing surface are at different angles. Mary used the Japanese technique of showing the same object from different viewpoints.

# In the Omnibus

**The mother's** face is drawn with bold, black outlines.

This image shows passengers in a horse-drawn omnibus, or bus. It is another print from the "Set of Ten" from 1891. In her first drawings of the scene, Mary included a man and another woman. She decided to leave them out and just show this small group.

Mary is famous for her pictures of mothers and children. Here the child's mother looks out of the window at the river while a nanny looks after the child. The dark, straight lines on the women's dresses are made with a technique called drypoint. The bigger colored areas on the dresses are created with aquatint.

**Mary liked** to show details from everyday life. This type of baby clothing was worn by both boys and girls.

## In the Frame

🔹 The original print of *In the Omnibus* is 14.5 inches (36.8 cm) tall and 10.5 inches (26 cm) wide.

🔹 Mary printed 25 copies of the finished picture.

There are two ways for a painter: the broad and easy one or the narrow and hard one.

**This is** a bridge over the Seine River, in the center of Paris. Mary usually painted women in their homes.

**This woman's** hat is much smaller than the other woman's. This means she is probably the child's nanny.

## CASSATT'S
## Palette of the picture

# The Boating Party

Mary painted this picture in 1893 or 1894 while she was on holiday in the south of France. The bright colors and lack of shadows suggest the strong Mediterranean sunlight.

Mary probably got the idea for this subject from *Boating*, a painting by Édouard Manet. Manet was one of her favorite artists. Mary told her friends, the Havemeyers, that they should buy his picture. She told them it was "the last word in painting," meaning that it was the best. The design of Mary's own picture is bold and lifelike.

## In the Frame

🖌 The original painting of *The Boating Party* is 35.5 inches (90.2 cm) tall and 46.25 inches (117.5 cm) wide.

🖌 Mary included the painting in her first major US exhibition in 1895.

**Mary paints** from a very low angle. She cuts the boat off at the frame to make the viewer feel like a passenger in the boat.

**The horizon** line at the top of the picture helps to bring our eyes to the woman in the boat.

**The woman** and child look at the rower. Is this a family outing, or is the rower a hired boatman?

CASSATT'S

Palette of the picture

**Mary did not** often paint men. At the time, a woman artist would not have been allowed to be alone with a male model in the studio.

# Family Group Reading

Mary painted this picture in 1898. It was bought by her friend Louisine Havemeyer. They had met in Paris when Louisine was a young student. Louisine later married a wealthy businessman.

Mary taught Louisine about art. She helped the Havemeyers build up a large art collection. Louisine eventually owned many paintings by Monet, Manet, and Degas. She also owned 20 of Mary's works. Louisine helped bring Impressionist paintings to the United States. Images of women and children reading were popular at the time.

### CASSATT'S

**Palette of the picture**

### In the Frame

The original painting of *Family Group Reading* is 22.25 inches (56.5 cm) tall and 44.25 inches (112.4 cm) wide.

**Mary was** good at painting children. She said: "I love to paint children. They are so natural and truthful."

**The mother's** face is painted with great attention to detail.

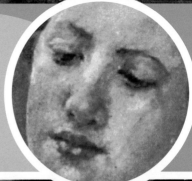

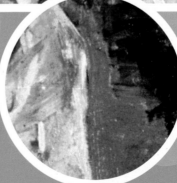

**The girl** rests both her hands on her mother's, as she holds the book open.

**The sky** can only really be seen reflected in the water.

# What Came Next?

Mary Cassatt helped to make Impressionism popular, especially in the United States. She also helped to make it more acceptable for women to be artists.

There were not many female Impressionist painters. Like her male friends, Mary wanted to paint scenes from everyday life. The male Impressionists often painted in bars and cafés in Paris. A woman could not go to such places without causing outrage. Instead, Mary chose to paint the lives of women like herself. Her paintings show people going to the theater, driving a carriage, having fittings with a dressmaker, taking care of their children, or visiting with friends.

## Famous Women Artists

- Sonia Delaunay
- Gwen John
- Frida Kahlo
- Tamara de Lempicka
- Margaret MacDonald
- Berthe Morisot
- Georgia O'Keeffe
- Suzanne Valadon

After Mary's career, it was easier for women to become artists. The Welsh painter Gwen John spent most of her life working in France.

**Gwen John**
*Young Woman Holding a Black Cat*, c.1920.

Mary also helped to make the work of the Impressionists popular. The Cassatts were wealthy, so Mary knew other wealthy Americans. She persuaded them to buy her friends' paintings and leave them to museums in their wills. This helped the Impressionists sell more pictures at higher prices. Many members of the group made enough money to live on.

Mary also helped other women artists. In 1892, she was asked to create a huge mural, or wall painting, for the World's Columbian Exposition in Chicago. This was an important international art exhibition. Mary's mural decorated the Women's Building, and she chose a subject that summed up her own life and work: *Modern Woman*.

Frederick Childe Hassam was another American Impressionist. Like Mary, he helped to make Impressionism popular outside Europe.

**Childe Hassam**
*Celia Thaxter's Garden*, 1890.

# How to Paint Like Cassatt

Painting exactly like Mary is very hard. She trained at art school for years. But it is still fun to try painting the same kinds of subjects that Mary enjoyed painting.

## WHAT YOU'LL NEED:

- a photograph (to copy)

- a pencil

- thick white paper or cardboard

- colored crayons

- small brushes

- acrylic paints

**1.**

Find a photograph to copy. Perhaps it could be of you and your mom when you were little or of you and your brothers and sisters.

**2.**

Using a pencil, lightly sketch the shapes from the photograph onto a piece of stiff white paper or cardboard.

**3.**

Outline the shapes of your drawing with colored crayons. This was a technique Mary used when she made prints. Do not worry if the lines are not completely clear. You can go over the same part again and again until it looks right.

**4.**

Use paints to fill in the color and detail of your drawing. Mary liked lighter colors. She also knew that you don't have to fill in every detail. If you prefer, leave parts of the picture such as the background so they are quite sketchy. This will make them look more Impressionistic, like the paintings of Mary's friends.

# Timeline

- **1844:** Born in Allegheny City, Pennsylvania, USA.

- **1851:** Moves to Europe for 4 years.

- **1861:** Studies at the Pennsylvania Academy of Fine Arts in Philadelphia.

- **1866:** Moves to Paris to study art.

- **1870:** Leaves Paris because of the Franco–Prussian War.

- **1873:** Returns to settle in Paris.

- **1877:** Meets Edgar Degas, who introduces her to the Impressionists.

- **1879:** Exhibits paintings at the Impressionists' exhibition.

- **1892:** Paints *Modern Woman* for an international exhibition in Chicago.

- **1926:** Dies after a long illness.

# Glossary

**aquatint:** A form of printing that uses colored powder to create different effects.

**drypoint engraving:** A form of printing in which the artist scratches lines into a wax covering on a metal plate to create a picture.

**etching:** A design made by scratching a drawing on a metal plate.

**mural:** A large painting that is painted directly onto a wall or another surface.

**palette:** The range of colors an artist uses in a particular painting or group of paintings.

**plate:** A flat piece of copper or other metal on which a design is drawn in order to create a print.

**print:** An image that is drawn on a sheet of metal or other material so that it can be covered in ink and pressed onto a sheet of paper to produce a picture.

**sketch:** A rough drawing that is often done in preparation for making a larger painting.

**traditional:** Something that has been done in the same way for a long time.

**viewpoint:** The position in which someone stands to see a particular scene.

# Further information

## BOOKS

Casey, Carolyn. *Mary Cassatt: The Life of an Artist* (Artist Biographies). Enslow Publishers Inc, 2004.

Harris, Lois. *Mary Cassatt: Impressionist Painter*. Pelican Publishing, 2007.

Hoena, Blake A. *Mary Cassatt* (Masterpieces: Artists and their Works). Bridgestone Books, 2003.

Mattern, Joanne. *Mary Cassatt* (Great Artists). Checkerboard Library, 2005.

Merberg, Julie. *Quiet Time with Cassatt* (Mini-Masters). Chronicle Books, 2006.

Metropolitan Museum of Art. *Baby Loves*. Atheneum, 2003.

O'Connor, Jane. *Mary Cassatt: Family Pictures* (Smart ABout Art). Turtleback, 2003.

## MUSEUMS

You can see Mary's famous paintings from this book in these museums:

*Young Woman Sewing in a Garden*
Musée d'Orsay, Paris, France

*At the Opéra*
Museum of Fine Arts, Boston

*The Child's Bath*
Art Institute of Chicago

*The Letter*
There are numerous copies of this print. One is in the Worcester Art Museum, Worcester, Massachusetts

*In the Omnibus*
There are numerous copies of this print. One is in the National Gallery of Art, Washington, DC

*The Boating Party*
National Gallery of Art, Washington, DC

*Family Group Reading*
Philadelphia Museum of Art

## WEBSITES

http://www.nga.gov/kids/scoop-cassatt.pdf
A pull-out about Mary from the National Gallery of Art in Washington.

http://www.marycassatt.org/
An online gallery of all of Mary's works.

http://makingartfun.com/htm/f-maf-art-library/mary-cassatt-biography.htm
"Hey Kids, Meet Mary Cassatt," from Making Art Fun.

http://totallyhistory.com/mary-cassatt/
A biography of Mary on the Totally History website.

# Index

# LIFE IN THE
# DESERTS

Author: **Lucy Baker**

Consultant: Roger Hammond,
*Director of Living Earth*

Published in the United States and Canada by
World Book, Inc.
233 N. Michigan Ave.
Suite 2000
Chicago, IL USA 60601
in association with Two-Can Publishing.

© Two-Can Publishing, 1997, 1990

**For information on other World Book products, call 1-800-WORLDBK (967-5325),
or visit us at our Web site at http://www.worldbook.com**

ISBN: 0-7166-5200-5 (hc)
LC: 96-61738

Text and design by Lucy Baker

Printed in Hong Kong

2 3 4 5 6 7 8 9 10 01 00 (hc)

# CONTENTS

# LOOKING AT THE DESERTS

There are places where rain hardly ever falls and few plants can survive, where the sun scorches the earth and strong winds whip sand and dust from the ground. These places are called **deserts**. But not all deserts are areas of shifting sands and intense heat. In fact, rock and gravel cover the greater part of most deserts. Some deserts, such as the Gobi Desert in Asia, are actually cold for most of the year. Other deserts are blisteringly hot during the day, but temperatures drop dramatically during the night.

A surprising variety of plant and animal life struggles to survive the harsh conditions of the desert, and many people call it their home.

▶ Some of the highest sand dunes in the world can be found in the Namib Desert in southern Africa. Sand dunes are not fixed features of the desert. They are mobile mounds of sand that are shaped by the wind.

▼ Death Valley, California, is the hottest, driest area of the United States.

▼ A boulder-strewn part of the Namib Desert shows signs of life after a good year's rainfall.

# WHERE IN THE WORLD?

Deserts cover about one-fifth of all the land in the world. There are deserts in parts of Africa, Asia, Australia, and North and South America.

Most deserts lie along two imaginary lines north and south of the equator, called the **Tropic of Cancer** and the **Tropic of Capricorn**. Here, and in other desert regions, dry air currents blow across the land. These dry air currents can blow hot or cold, but they rarely carry rain clouds. Consequently, the lands they cross are starved of rain and given no protection from the sun.

This map shows the main desert areas of the world. Do you live near desert lands?

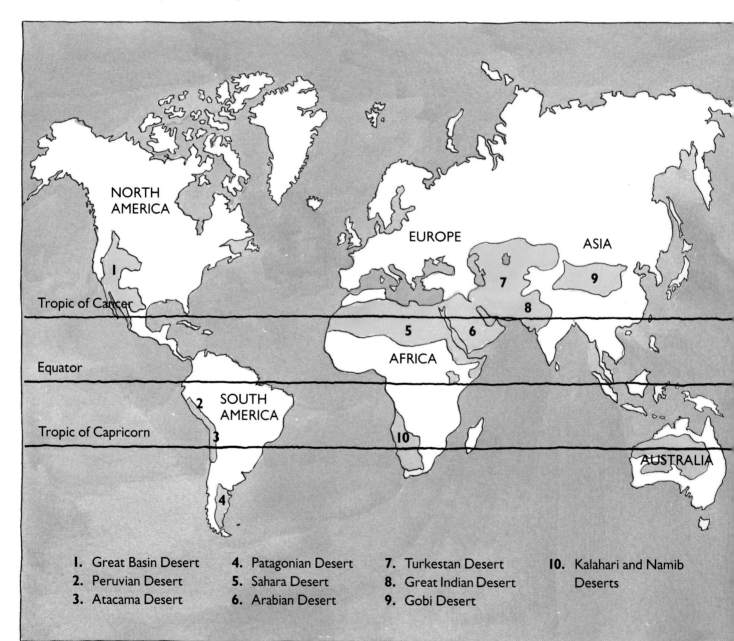

1. Great Basin Desert
2. Peruvian Desert
3. Atacama Desert
4. Patagonian Desert
5. Sahara Desert
6. Arabian Desert
7. Turkestan Desert
8. Great Indian Desert
9. Gobi Desert
10. Kalahari and Namib Deserts

# RAIN SHADOWS

Some deserts are called rain shadow deserts. These occur where large mountains block the path of rain-bearing wind. The raised mountain ground pushes the wind upward and as it rises, it cools. The drop in temperature causes clouds carried by the wind to burst and release their rain. The wind continues over the mountains, but by the time it reaches the other side it carries no rain clouds. This natural process creates some of the world's wettest environments—rain forests—alongside the world's driest.

The Sahara in northern Africa is the largest desert in the world. It covers an area roughly the size of the United States.

The Gobi Desert in eastern Asia is situated on high, windy plains. It is the coldest desert in the world.

Nearly half of Australia is covered by desert.

The Arabian Desert is the sandiest desert in the world.

The smallest desert regions of the world are the Peruvian and Atacama deserts on the western coast of South America.

Many of the world's deserts are bordered by areas of scant vegetation. These **scrublands** would become true deserts if they were to lose their native trees and plants.

▲ Ancient rock paintings in African and Asian deserts show giraffes, antelope, and other grazing animals that could not survive in today's desert conditions. This suggests that the lands were once more **fertile**. Evidence of ancient lakes and forests can also be found in the world's deserts.

# DESERT PLANTS

It is astonishing that any plants have learned to survive in desert conditions. Most plants rely on regular rainfall, but desert plants may have to go without fresh water for more than a year. In addition, many desert plants have to cope with both hot and cold temperatures, as each boiling day turns into another freezing night.

Some desert plants remain hidden in the ground as seeds until rain falls. By waiting until conditions are good, they do not have to cope with the rigors of desert life.

▼ The gigantic welwitschia plant is unique to the Namib Desert. This desert has a rare water source—fogs that drift across it from the coast. The welwitschia's leaves absorb tiny particles of water from the foggy air.

▲ Cacti are the most famous desert plants. They are native to North and South American deserts, but they have been introduced to other parts of the world.

Prickly pear cacti were taken to Australia and planted as hedges around homes in the outback. They grew so quickly that large areas were overrun by the spiky plants. Small creatures that eat the prickly pear's soft insides had to be introduced to Australia to help reclaim the land.

Cacti are flowering plants. Some cacti produce flowers every year, while others rarely come into blossom. Birds visit cacti to extract sugary nectar from their flowers or search their stems for insects.

The cactus in this picture is a giant saguaro. Saguaro cacti can grow to nearly 50 feet (15 meters) in height and may hold several tons (kilograms) of water in their swollen stems. Like other cacti, the saguaro has no leaves. Instead, prickly spines grow around its stem. These spines create a layer of still air around the surface of the plant and so protect it from drying winds.

# SURVIVAL TRICKS

Desert plants have special ways of surviving without regular rainfall. Some suck up as much water as they can during occasional rains and then store it in their stems or leaves. Here are some other ways desert plants collect and conserve water.

Some desert trees have long **taproots**, which grow deep into the ground to reach underground water sources.

Many plants, like the creosote bush, have a vast network of shallow roots to extract every available drop of moisture from their patch of the desert.

Some desert plants store food and water underground in thickened roots, bulbs, or **tubers**. The stems of such plants, exposed to sun and wind, may look dead, but as soon as it rains they spring into life, producing leaves, fruits, and flowers.

# HIDDEN LIFE

It is difficult to believe that hundreds of different animals live in deserts. Most of the time, these are quiet, still places. This is because many desert creatures move around only at dawn or dusk. At other times of the day, they burrow underground or hide beneath rocks or plants to avoid very hot or cold conditions.

The animals living in the desert rely on plant life and on each other for their survival. Roots, stems, leaves, and seeds form the basic diet of many desert creatures, and they, in turn, are hunted by other animals. The largest hunters in the desert include wild cats, foxes, and wolves.

Some desert creatures get all the water they need from the food they eat. Others have to travel long distances to visit rare water holes.

▲ Scorpions hunt spiders, insects, and other sma animals on the desert floor. Once they have caug their meal, they use the poisonous stings at the end of their tails to kill their prey. People stung b a scorpion usually suffer just a sharp pain, but the most powerful scorpion stings can be deadly.

▼ Many reptiles are successful desert dwellers, especially snakes and lizards. Some snakes have a special way of moving across shifting sands. They throw their heads to one side and their bodies follow in a loop. This is called sidewinding. Snake can also burrow into the sand to cool down or escape from predators.

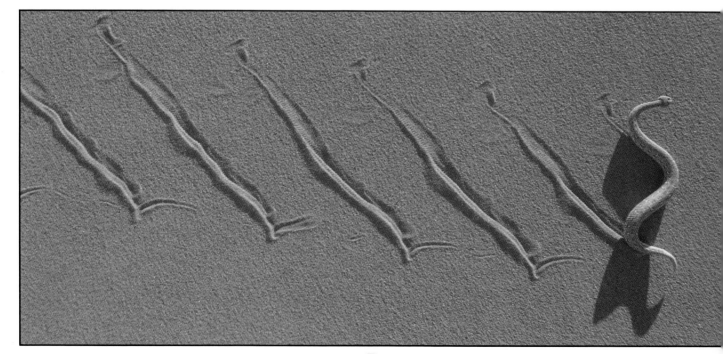

Rabbits, gerbils, and many other small mammals live in desert lands. The cottontail rabbit, right, can be found in some American deserts. It has large ears that act as radiators, giving off heat and so helping the rabbit to cool down.

Many lizards live in the world's deserts. Like other reptiles, they have a scaly skin that stops them from drying up in the baking sunshine. Most lizards are insect-eaters. They chase flies or sit patiently waiting for a beetle or a line of ants to pass them by. Lizards have many enemies, so they must stay on their guard. The horned lizard, below, has excellent camouflage that makes it hard to find on the desert floor.

# CROSSING THE DESERT

The largest desert animals do not remain in one area of the desert. They travel long distances in search of food and water. Small numbers of antelope, goats, and sheep are found in most deserts of the world. A rare horse, called Przewalski's horse, once roamed the cold Gobi Desert but is now thought to be **extinct** in the wild.

The most famous animal to cross the desert is the camel. The camel is sometimes called the ship of the desert, because it can travel over vast seas of inhospitable rock and sand better than any other animal.

There are two kinds of camels. The dromedary has one hump on its back and a thin coat. It is native to the hot deserts of Arabia and North Africa, but it also has been introduced to parts of America and Australia. The Bactrian camel has two humps and a darker, thicker coat than its cousin. It comes from the cooler central Asian deserts.

Camels are well built for desert life. They have bushy eyebrows and two rows of eyelashes to help keep the sand out of their eyes. Their slit nostrils can be closed for the same reason. Their two-toed feet spread out as they walk and stop them from sinking into the sand.

The humps on camels' backs do not contain water as was once believed. They hold fat reserves that can be broken down into food when camels are crossing the desert. If a camel is starving, its hump will shrink.

# DID YOU KNOW?

● Less than 100 years ago, it was impossible to cross the vast Sahara and Arabian deserts without the help of a camel. Today cars and trucks are used for many desert journeys, and camels are becoming less important to the lives of desert people.

● Thirsty camels can drink up to 30 gallons (140 liters) of water in one sitting and then go for more than a week without water.

● Camels are the domestic animals of the desert. They are used as transportation. They provide meat and milk for food. Their hairy coats are woven into cloth. Even the camel's dry droppings are used as fuel for cooking fires.

# WHEN WATER FALLS

Some deserts have regular rainy seasons, but others may not see rain for many years. In the desert there are only torrential downpours. Violent desert rainstorms cause flash floods and destruction. Plants are washed away, and some animals drown.

Rain brings life as well as death to desert lands. Days after a heavy storm, billions of tiny seeds spring to life on the desert floor. These small flowering plants, called **ephemerals**, have been hiding in the sand since the last rainfall. Millions of insect eggs are also brought to life by the drumming rain, and so an army of flies, bees, and wasps appears. These insects feed on the ephemerals and help them to reproduce by spreading pollen from flower to flower.

Eight weeks after the rain, the desert is empty again. The colorful flowers and buzzing insects have gone. But millions and billions of new seeds and eggs now lie hidden in the desert sands. Many of them will be eaten by permanent desert dwellers, but some are bound to survive until the next rain comes and the life cycle can be repeated.

▶ Lightning strikes as a storm passes over the Sonoran Desert in North America. A whole year's rainfall can come in one single cloudburst.

▲ Colorful, flowering plants brighten the sandy Arabian Desert after a recent rainfall.

## DID YOU KNOW?

● Sometimes rainstorms fail to wet the desert floor. If it is very hot when a storm occurs, the rain may turn into vapor before it reaches the ground. More than 12 inches (30 centimeters) of rain may fall during one heavy storm in the desert.

● The Atacama Desert is the driest in the world. Some parts of it experienced a 400-year drought until 1971.

# DESERT PEOPLE

The desert is a dangerous place for people not used to its hostile conditions. Even so, a few people call the open desert home.

The **Bushmen** of the Kalahari Desert in southern Africa are **nomads**, which means that they travel from place to place. Bushmen survive by hunting wild game and gathering edible plants and insects. Some Aborigines once lived this way in the heart of Australia's desert lands, but most are now settled in goverment-funded camps.

The world's most barren deserts such as the Sahara, Arabian, and Gobi deserts do not have enough native plants and animals to support **hunter-gatherers**. Instead, the nomadic people take from the desert what they can but also kill or trade animals such as goats, sheep, or camels for food.

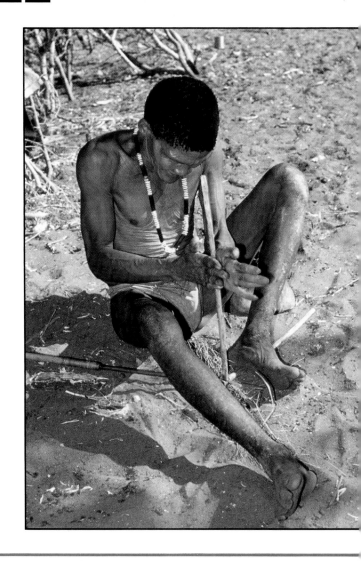

## PEOPLE FACTS

Bushmen rarely drink. They get most of the water they need from plant roots and desert melons found on or under the desert floor.

The turban worn by many desert people is not a hat. It is a very long piece of cloth that is wrapped around and around the head. It helps to keep desert sand out of the eyes, nose, and mouth.

People in the cold Gobi Desert live in sturdy, round huts called yurts. These simple homes can withstand winds up to 90 miles (145 kilometers) an hour.

These men belong to a group of people called the Tuareg. The Tuareg were once known as the pirates of the desert. For many years they controlled trade across the Sahara by patrolling the desert on racing camels.

A Bushman of the Kalahari makes a fire by rubbing two sticks together. Bushmen have their own special language that includes clicking sounds. Bushmen live in huts built from local materials. The frame is made of branches, and the roof is thatched with long grass.

Many desert nomads live in tents, like the one in this picture. When it is time to move on, the nomads pack up the tent. It is then carried by a camel or donkey.

# DESERT OASES

In parts of the desert, plants grow in abundance and water is available throughout the year. These places are called oases.

Most oases are fed by underground pools of water that formed over thousands of years. The water is trapped between layers of rock below the desert floor. Rivers also create oases. The largest oasis in the world lies along the banks of the great River Nile, which flows through the Sahara.

Oases are the most densely populated areas of the desert. The regular water supply makes it possible for people to settle permanently and build villages, towns, or cities. The land is **irrigated**, and date palms, olives, wheat, millet, and other food crops are grown.

▲ If seasonal rains fail, water must be carried to the fields to keep desert crops alive.

Many desert towns are built from materials of the desert itself. Mud is mixed with straw and water to make bricks, which are then baked in the sun. This village is the home of the Dogon. Dogon people get their water from nearby mountain pools. The Dogons live in Mali, which is in northern Africa.

Oases are like green islands surrounded by a sea of sand and rock. Animals and people alike depend on oases for their drinking water.

Oases do not last forever. The world's deserts are littered with ghost towns, where the water has run dry or the oasis has been swamped by shifting sand dunes. In such places the people have moved on.

# CREEPING DESERTS

The world's deserts are growing. Through a process known as **desertification**, scrub and grasslands become as dry and barren as the deserts they border. At the present rate of desertification, more than 77,220 square miles (200,000 square kilometers) of new desert land throughout the world are created every year.

Deserts naturally shrink and grow depending on the amount of rain they receive. In recent years, however, widespread droughts have caused deserts to grow at an alarming rate.

Scientists believe the droughts are par of a worldwide change in weather patterns caused by pollution in the atmosphere.

Desert nomads speed up the process of desertification by cutting down trees and grazing their animals on threatened grasslands. This leaves the land exposed to sun, wind, and occasional violent rains. The delicate **topsoil** dries out then is blown and washed away.

Intensive farming can also cause desertification. The pressure to grow

more and more food on the same amount of land encourages farmers to overwork the soil, and this can have disastrous consequences. In the 1930's, intensive farming and grazing in America's southern states created a huge area of bare and desertlike land called the Dust Bowl. Droughts had dried up the soil, and winds then carried it away. Cities hundreds of miles away were plunged into darkness as huge clouds of dust blew across the sky.

▼ If the ground cover is removed from dry scrublands, the hot sun bakes the earth. Rains run straight off the hard ground, and any remaining trees weaken and die.

## DID YOU KNOW?

More than 400 million short tons (363 million metric tons) of African soil is blown west over the Atlantic Ocean every year. In 1988 hundreds of tiny, pink Saharan frogs rained down on a British village during a bad storm.

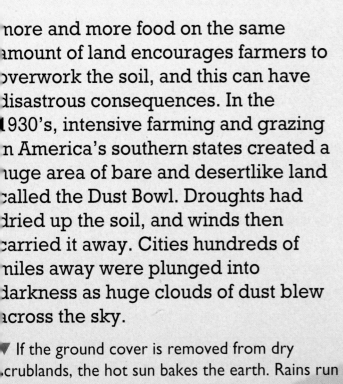

# DESERTS TODAY

For centuries the world's deserts were regarded as terrifying wastelands. They remained the exclusive property of small desert tribes who managed to survive in hostile conditions. Only recently has the arrival of cars, trucks, and airplanes expanded the possibilities for desert exploration.

Today industries are active in the desert. Mining companies use massive machinery to extract rich mineral reserves such as copper, iron, salt, and uranium. Oil is also found in some deserts and has brought great wealth to certain areas. Saudi Arabia holds some of the world's largest oil fields.

Elsewhere, modern technology has been used to turn the desert green. By finding new underground water sources or by tapping nearby rivers, people can grow crops on desert land.

Desertification is a problem in many areas of the world, but Africa is the most obvious victim. In some African countries, crops have failed for several years running, which has caused widespread **famine**. Many nomads have cast off their ancient ways of life, as lengthy droughts have left the desert bare.

◀ As rich countries transform their deserts into farmland, poorer African countries try to hold back the creeping edge of the Sahara. This man is building simple rock walls to prevent the seasonal rains from running straight off the hard ground.

## DID YOU KNOW?

● Today **arid** lands produce one-fifth of the world's food supply. By 2000, one-third of all farmland may be desert if the soil is overworked.

● Satellite pictures can locate hidden water pools under the desert floor. Modern drilling equipment can then reach the water to create new oases.

▲ Oil flares send smoke plumes into the desert air.

▶ Plastic tunnels cover healthy desert crops. The tunnels prevent precious water from **evaporating** into the dry desert air. Continual evaporation may encourage salts to rise to the surface of the desert. These salts kill most plant life and poison the soil.

# JEALOUS GOOMBLE-GUBBON

*For thousands of years people have told stories about the world around them. Often these stories try to explain something that people do not really understand, like how the world began or where light comes from. This tale is told by the Aboriginal people of Australia.*

Long ago in Australia was the Dream Time when everything was made. The land was made, with mountains, plains, and valleys full of all sorts of animals, birds, and plants. And the sea was made, full of whales, dolphins, and plants. But there were not yet any fish.

All the birds had been given wonderful and extraordinary voices: Crow croaked his rasping caw, Kookaburra laughed her hilarious chuckle, and the other birds sang in all their different voices. They sat singing in the trees and bushes all day long, because they were so happy.

When I say they all had wonderful and extraordinary voices, I am forgetting Goomble-Gubbon, the turkey. Goomble-Gubbon could only make a low bubbling noise in his throat, which sounded like this: "goomble gubbon, goomble gubbon." All the other birds thought Goomble-Gubbon's voice was a great joke, and they sang even more beautifully when he was around just to tease him.

Of course, they didn't really mean to be cruel. They were all so happy themselves that they did not realize how much they were hurting poor Goomble-Gubbon's feelings. They were very fond of him in spite of his bad-tempered ways.

Goomble-Gubbon did not find his voice funny. He thought it was terrible, and he was very jealous of all the other birds' voices. He tried everything he could to improve his voice, but nothing was any use. If only the other birds' voices were not so wonderful and extraordinary, his voice would not seem so terrible, he thought.

One day was worse than ever before. The other birds had been laughing at Goomble-Gubbon all morning, and he was tired of it. So he went off to visit his friend Lizard. Lizard never laughed at his voice. The two of them sat talking and telling stories until the sun began to set. Just then, Kookaburra flew into the branches of a nearby tree and began to laugh.

Now, Kookaburra could not help laughing. She laughed at everything, even at things that were not at all funny, and Goomble-Gubbon should have known this really. But he was fed up with being teased by all the other birds, and so he thought that Kookaburra had flown over and perched on that very branch just to laugh at him.

"What do you think you're laughing at?" he snapped angrily.

Kookaburra looked most surprised and flew off to tell the other birds about Goomble-Gubbon's strange behavior.

Meanwhile Goomble-Gubbon made up his mind to put a stop to the other birds' teasing once and for all. He waited until it was dark and all the birds were asleep in the trees. Then, very quietly, he went to the magic burning tree. This was a tree where men took their firesticks to fetch fire for food, warmth, and light for their camps. Goomble-Gubbon picked up a stick from the ground and lit it from the tree. Then he crept around to all the trees and bushes where the birds were sleeping and set the bottom branches alight.

"That should get rid of those nasty laughing birds," he thought to himself gleefully. "Now I'll have the most beautiful voice of all."

However, Kookaburra was not asleep. She heard Goomble-Gubbon creeping around beneath the trees and woke the other birds to warn them.

A great swarm of birds rose up from the trees, screeching and crying. The birds who could fly fast flew away as quickly as they could to far-off places where there was no fire. Those who could not fly fast enough to get away from the flames flew into the sea to cool off. As they entered the water, their wings turned into fins and their feathers became scales. At last there were fish in the sea!

Goomble-Gubbon was furious that his plan had not worked. He waved the firestick wildly, but he managed only to singe his own feathers a nasty smoky color and burn his head bright red too. He threw the firestick far out into the bush.

The fire in the trees went on burning until the land in the center of Australia was quite barren and dry. And that is how the desert came to be in the center of Australia. All because of jealous Goomble-Gubbon.

# TRUE OR FALSE?

Which of these facts are true and which ones are false? If you have read this book carefully, you will know the answers.

1. All deserts are very hot.
2. Deserts receive no rain at all during the year.
3. The Gobi Desert is the largest desert in the world.
4. Nights in the desert are extremely cold.

5. Lush rain forests can lie alongside rain shadow deserts.
6. Saguaro cacti can grow close to 50 feet (15 meters) high.

7. The ears of the American cottontail rabbit act as radiators.

8. A camel's humps are used to store water.

9. The dromedary has two humps and a thick coat.
10. The Tuareg were once known as the pirates of the desert.
11. Many desert towns are built from mud bricks.
12. In 1988 thousands of large blue fish rained down on a British village during a bad storm.

Answers: 1. False 2. False 3. False 4. True 5. True 6. True 7. True 8. False 9. Fasle 10. True 11. True 12. False.

# GLOSSARY

● **Arid** land is parched soil with sparse vegetation. Little rain falls on this type of land and it is prone to desertification.

● **Bushmen** are people who live in desert lands such as in Africa or Australia. They drink little, as they obtain enough moisture from eating underground roots and desert melons.

● **Desert** is a place with little vegetation where less than 10 inches (25 centimeters) of rain falls each year.

● **Desertification** is the process by which dry areas of land on the edge of deserts suffer from drought and also become desert. If regular rainfall returns to the area, the new region of desert could recover.

● **Domesticated** animals are those which have been bred by humans over many generations to be tame and to provide products such as meat, milk, leather, and wool.

● **Drought** is a period when very little or no rain falls. Crops do not grow, water is scarce, and animals and humans find it hard to survive.

● **Ephemerals** are tiny plants that survive as seeds in dry conditions such as desert sands. They wait for a period of heavy rain and then burst into flower.

● **Evaporation** is when water turns into tiny droplets of vapor in the air. This process happens each morning to the dew that has fallen during the night in the hot desert.

● **Extinct** means that the last member of an animal or plant species has died out as a result of overhunting, a change in its habitat, or its failure to compete with a new animal or plant.

● **Famine** is a period when food is scarce and many people and animals starve and die. This usually takes place after wartime or after a drought, when crops have been unable to grow.

● **Fertile** land is that which is good for growing lush and healthy crops.

● **Hunter-gatherers** are people who live off the land by harvesting food from the plants and animals that live there. They are skillful in taking only what the land can survive without.

**Irrigation** is the method by which farmers water land that naturally tends to be dry. Water is often channeled over land through ditches or retained on land with a hard, resistant surface such as low walls.

**Nomads** are people who travel from one area to another either to take their herds of animals to fresh grazing or to escape severe weather such as cold or drought. They feed mainly on products from their herds and live in tents, which can easily be packed up and carried on the next journey.

● **Scrubland** is territory where vegetation grows low and stunted.

● **Taproots** are long, thin roots that push their way through the layers of stone beneath the sand. They help some desert trees find moisture during long periods of drought.

● **Topsoil** is the uppermost and richest layer of earth where most plants grow. The desert lacks topsoil, which has dried out with lack of rain and has blown away.

● **Tubers** are short, thick parts of underground stems of certain plants. They are covered in small bumps.

● **Tropic of Cancer** and **Tropic of Capricorn** are imaginary lines at about 23°27″ north and south of the equator. Most deserts are found along these two lines.

# INDEX